SHEET MUSIC *for* PIANO

Brahms

Intermediate to Advanced Piano Masterpieces

MP3s
ONLINE LINKS
Resources

Alan Brown

With an Introduction by Malcolm MacDonald

FLAME TREE
PUBLISHING

FLAME TREE
PIANO KEYBOARD

Publisher and Creative Director: Nick Wells
Project Editors: Laura Bulbeck & Polly Prior
Music Transcription: Alan Brown
Introductory Text: Malcolm MacDonald

This edition first published 2015 by
FLAME TREE PUBLISHING
Crabtree Hall, Crabtree Lane
Fulham, London SW6 6TY
United Kingdom
www.flametreepublishing.com
www.flametreemusic.com

Website for this book: www.flametreepiano.com

© 2015 Flame Tree Publishing Ltd

15 17 19 18 16
1 3 5 7 9 10 8 6 4 2

ISBN 978-1-78361-424-0

A CIP record for this book is available from the British Library upon request.

Alan Brown (Music Transcription)
A former member of the Scottish National Orchestra, Alan now works as a freelance
musician, with several leading UK orchestras, and as a consultant in music and IT. Alan has
had several compositions published, developed a set of music theory CD-Roms, co-written a
series of Bass Guitar Examination Handbooks and worked on over 100 further titles.

Malcolm MacDonald (Introductory Text)
Malcolm MacDonald edited *Tempo*, the quarterly magazine of modern music, and was a
freelance writer on music and broadcaster. His books included *Brahms* and *Schoenberg*
in the Master Musicians series, a study of the music of Edgard Varèse and volumes on the
British composers Havergal Brian, John Foulds and Ronald Stevenson. He died in 2014.

Printed in China

Contents

How to Use the Website

The Flame Tree Piano and Keyboard website (www.flametreepiano. com) offers a number of significant benefits for readers and users of this sheet music book. It can be accessed on a desktop computer (Mac or PC), tablet (such as the iPad or Nexus) or any internet enabled smartphone.

The Home Page

With a series of options the website allows the reader to find out more, both about the composer and the music. Biographies, mp3s and further resources are provided to allow you to explore the subject further.

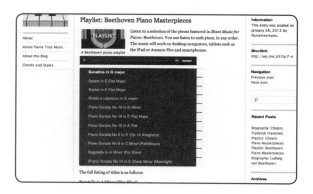

The Audio Player

The primary tool on the website is the use of an audio player. All the pieces are presented to help you understand each of the masterpieces in this book. The simple play ▶ button allows you to play each piece through the speakers on your device. Although the music cannot be downloaded it is streamed, and is provided free of charge.

Life and Works

This book of sheet music pieces for the piano is introduced with a short guide to the composer. The website presents a more extensive text on the life, works, style and context, with information extracted from *The Classical Music Encyclopedia* (Flame Tree Publishing), edited by Stanley Sadie

(1930–2005), with a foreword by Vladimir Ashkenazy. Music editor for *The Times* for 17 years and editor of the standard classical music reference work *The New Grove Dictionary of Music and Musicians*, Stanley Sadie was, amongst many other achievements, president of the Royal Musical Association and the International Musicological Society. (*The Classical Music Encyclopedia* will be republished online and made available as a downloadable pdf, from www.flametreepiano.com.)

Free eBook

Created to complement this new series of books we have made a special edition, 96 page ebook, *Romantic Composers*. Featuring the primary composers, musicians and musical artists of the Romantic Era, the ebook can be downloaded onto any computer, tablet or smartphone and is an invaluable source of reference on a key period of musical history.

Other Features

The experience of playing the piano is one of constant development. To help with further discoveries we have provided a number of additional resources. Separate menus offer recommendations for further reading (books and online) and particular recordings.

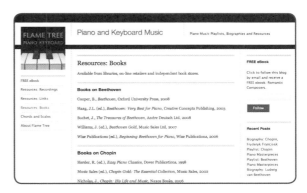

Introduction to Brahms

JOHANNES BRAHMS (1833–97) is a Janus-like figure in music history: he simultaneously faced the past and the future. Reviving and enlarging the classical principles of Haydn, Mozart and Beethoven, his music has often been seen as a conservative reaction against the 'new music' of Liszt and, in particular, Wagner. Yet Brahms's highly personal blend of Beethovenian dynamism, Schubertian lyricism and German folksong with the strict contrapuntal disciplines of the Baroque era, created a powerful new musical synthesis. His example was just as vital as Wagner's in the creation of the new music of the twentieth century. Though he appeared frequently as a pianist and conductor, after his thirties Brahms was financially successful enough to support himself as a freelance composer. Like Beethoven, he was a north German who based himself in Vienna, and remained a bachelor even though he was the centre of a large circle of influential musical friends.

Hamburg and Düsseldorf

Brahms, born on 7 May 1833 in a slum district of Hamburg, was the second of three children to Johann Jakob Brahms, a town musician, and Christiane Nissen, a seamstress. His musical talent was evident in early childhood; he grew up studying J. S. Bach with local piano teachers and playing in dockside taverns to augment the family's income. His first foray away from Hamburg in 1853–54 brought unexpected celebrity and the brief patronage of Robert Schumann. After Schumann's suicide attempt in February 1854, Brahms remained in Düsseldorf, helping Schumann's wife and family, until the older composer's death. During 1857–60 he divided his time mainly between Hamburg, where he conducted a women's choir, and an annual appointment at the small ducal court of Detmold. In 1858–59 Brahms spent time in Göttingen, where he became engaged to Agathe von Siebold, then almost immediately broke off the relationship. Although his music was becoming more widely known, he continued to base himself in Hamburg, evidently hoping to succeed the ageing conductor of the town orchestra, but while he was visiting Vienna for the first time in late 1862, the post was awarded to another.

Away From Hamburg

Brahms left Hamburg in April 1853 to work as accompanist to the Hungarian violinist Eduard Rémenyi (1830–98), who introduced him to his fellow-countryman Joachim, already recognized as the greatest violinist of the age. When Rémenyi decided to go his own way, Joachim gave Brahms introductions to Liszt and Schumann. A walking tour of the Rhineland brought Brahms to Düsseldorf at the end of September. Here Schumann was astounded by his compositions and forthwith arranged for some of them to be published in Leipzig by the end of the year. In an article for the influential journal *Neue Zeitschrift für Musik* he hailed Brahms as 'the chosen one … destined to give the highest expression to the times'. In February 1854, Schumann's madness, suicide attempt and subsequent incarceration in an asylum left Brahms without a patron, yet he chivalrously assumed the role of protector of Clara Schumann (1819–96) and her numerous children.

Friendships

Brahms was a solitary, difficult man, with a powerful need for friendship. Among his most significant relationships were those with Clara Schumann, widow of Robert Schumann, and the violinist-composer Joachim. Fourteen years his senior, Clara represented a romantic ideal of womanhood and was also one of the most gifted pianists of the century. Soon after their first meeting, Brahms realized he loved her. She returned his affection, though they are generally thought not to have been lovers. Clara's advocacy as a performer helped to make Brahms' piano music widely known. Relations with the touchy Joachim were more chequered, but he helped the young Brahms gain confidence in composition and did much, both as violinist and conductor, to promote Brahms' cause. Brahms wrote several important works for him, notably the Violin Concerto and Double Concerto.

Vienna, Life and Contacts

The lack of recognition Brahms had found in his home town contrasted with the warm welcome he encountered in Austria from such new friends as the influential critic Eduard Hanslick. He spent increasingly long periods in Vienna, and essentially settled there from 1863, when he accepted the conductorship of the Singakademie, for a year. For three seasons (1872–75) he directed the concert series of the *Gesellschaft der Musikfreunde* ('Society of the Friends of Music'), but a permanent post did not suit him and he lived otherwise as a freelance composer.

International Reputation

Brahms began to reach a mass audience with his waltzes and *Hungarian Dances* for piano duet, and with vocal quartets and songs. He was deeply affected by his mother's death and his major choral work, *Ein deutsches Requiem* ('A German Requiem'), was written partly in her memory, and laid the foundation of Brahms' international reputation. This work and the subsequent *Triumphlied* ('Song of Triumph') were much performed as patriotic music during the Franco-Prussian War, further enhancing his profile in Germany. Meanwhile, his profound chamber and instrumental works allowed him to master each genre in turn, approaching the summit of his ambitions: the symphony.

The 'Third B'

From the time of the First Symphony (1876) Brahms' place in European musical life was assured, and he received many public honours. In 1895 he was hailed as the 'third B' in a festival at Meiningen devoted to 'the three great B's – Bach, Beethoven and Brahms'. During his last 20 years, Brahms created his greatest masterpieces and established a fruitful relationship with the ducal orchestra in Meiningen. He aided many musicians out of his own purse and helped to further several notable careers, such as that of Dvořák. Brahms continued to travel widely, but this latter stage of his life was darkened by the deaths of many of his friends, and his music took on an increasingly elegiac character, for example in the autumnal Clarinet Quintet, and the *Vier ernste Gesänge* ('Four Serious Songs') to biblical texts, written after Clara Schumann's death in 1896. He died of cancer of the liver on 3 April 1897.

Looking To The Past

Brahms blended many influences into a potent and highly individual idiom. He felt that the programmatic music advocated by the 'New German School' was damaging the essentials of the art, and in 1860 he published an unsuccessful manifesto directed against Liszt and his followers – his only foray into public polemics. On the other hand, he admired Wagner, whereas Wagner resented Brahms' growing reputation and sought to belittle him as a mere academic. Brahms indeed was in the forefront of the nineteenth- century movement to arrive at a fuller and more accurate understanding of earlier masters, and studied their music more systematically than any composer before him.

Influences

The profound influence of Beethoven is obvious in the monumental First Piano Concerto and First Symphony, but Brahms was equally inspired by Mozart, Haydn and particularly Schubert, whose major works were only being rediscovered in the 1860s. Far more than most contemporaries, he was aware of George Frideric Handel (1685–1759) and J. S. Bach, whose music was gradually being published throughout the late nineteenth century. Moreover he collected, studied and performed music from the Renaissance and early Baroque periods, which taught him the value of strictly imitative contrapuntal forms such as canon and fugue. He also collected and arranged many German folksongs, which helped to develop his richly lyrical style of melody. This broad synthesis of influences, allied to his uniquely flexible sense of rhythm, created many new possibilities for the composers who came after him, notably Reger and Schoenberg.

Styles and Forms

Broadly speaking, the new musical aesthetic that emerged after 1848 placed a much stronger emphasis on the individuality of each owrk, its unique 'sound world'. The idea of music belonging to a genre in which forms and styles traditionally differed from one work to another, was fading fast. Not the least significant feature of Verdi's three great operas *Rigoletto*, *Il trouvatore* and *La traviata*, which marked his emergence in the early 1850s from this 'years in the galley' (as Verdi himself put it) with a new operatic realism and intensity of expression, was the fact that they were so different from one another. Each opera had its own highly individual vocal, instrumental and dramatic style. It is far from a coincidence, too, that in exactly the same period, Wagner publicly announced that he was going 'to write no more operas', by which he meant that the new works for the stage he was planning to compose were finally to be cut loose from opera's traditional moorings. Liszt's invention of the new 'genre' of the symphonic poem had the same ambition: each work turned out to have not just its own extramusical programme, but also its own form, thematic character, instrumentation and time-scale.

Serious and Popular Music

The reaction against this pronounced rejection of traditional style and form was twofold. First, the new generation of composers that began to emerge after mid- century, including Brahms, took the more conservative view that chamber music and the symphony were not as moribund as the New German School claimed they were. Secondly, the 'light' music written in vastly increasing quantities for the ballroom and the popular theatre relied for its effectiveness in part on a deliberately anti-progressive feature: an exaggerated sense of 'belonging' to a specific style and form. The elegant and highly successful waltzes of the Strauss family were an example, as were the neo-classical operettas of Offenbach, which were often open parodies of contemporary art music and its self-conscious efforts to be 'new'. Both the classical revival, which moved effortlessly from concert hall to drawing room, with familiar styles and forms specially prepared for 'easy' playing and listening, and the mass appeal of light music by composers such as Offenbach and Johann Strauss, helped to consolidate the widening gulf between the serious and the popular that characterized the music of the second half of the nineteenth century.

Ballades
(Op. 10, No. 1 in D Minor, Andante)

Tempo I

Deutsche Volkslieder

('Feinsliebchen, du solls', No. 12, WoO 33)

Delicamente e poco agitato

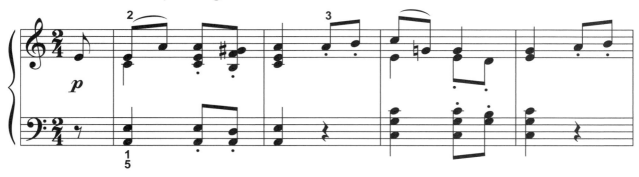

Eight Pieces
(Op. 76, No. 2 Capriccio in B Minor)

Allegretto non troppo

sempre leggiero

rit. e dim.

Eight Pieces
(Op. 76, No. 3 Intermezzo in A Flat Major)

Grazioso

Four Pieces for Piano
(Op. 119, No. 2 Intermezzo in E Minor)

Andantino un poco agitato

Andantino grazioso

Hungarian Dance
(WoO 1, No. 5 in F Sharp Minor)

Lullaby
('Wiegenlied', Op. 49, No. 4)

Dolce

Piano Sonata No. 2 in F Sharp Minor
(Op. 2, Allegro non Troppo)

Piano Sonata No. 3 in F Minor
(Op. 5, Andante Molto)

Adagio

Rhapsodies
(Op. 79, No. 2 in G Minor)

Molto passionato, ma non troppo allegro

Seven Fantasias
(Op. 116, No. 1 Capriccio in D Minor)

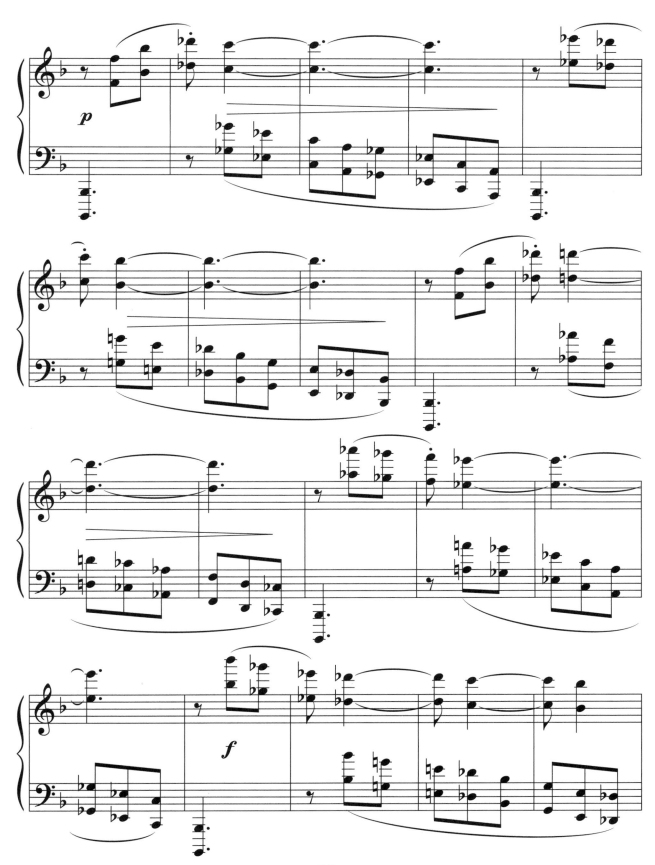

Seven Fantasias
(Op. 116, No. 6 Intermezzo in E Major)

Andantino teneremente

Six Pieces for Piano

(Op. 118, No. 1 Intermezzo in A Minor)

Allegro non assai, ma molto appassionato

Six Pieces for Piano
(Op. 118, No. 2 Intermezzo in A Major)

Andante teneramente

Six Pieces for Piano

(Op. 118, No. 3 Ballade in G Minor)

Six Pieces for Piano

(Op. 118, No. 5 Romanze in F Major)

Sixteen Waltzes

(Op 39, No. 1 in B Major)

Tempo giusto

Sixteen Waltzes
(Op. 39, No. 2 in E Major)

Sixteen Waltzes
(Op 39, No. 9 in D Minor)

Espressivo

Sixteen Waltzes
(Op 39, No. 10 in G Major)

Sixteen Waltzes
(Op 39, No. 11 in B Minor)

Allegretto

Sixteen Waltzes
(Op 39, No. 15 in A Flat Major)

Dolce

Three Intermezzi
(Op. 117, No. 1 in E Flat Major)

Three Intermezzi
(Op. 117, No. 2 in B Flat Minor)

Andante non troppo e con molto espressione

Three Intermezzi

(Op. 117, No. 3 in C Sharp Minor)

Andante con moto

Poco più lento

Più moto ed espressivo

Variations
(Op. 21, No. 1, Theme, Var. 1, Var. 2)

www.flametreepiano.com

Audio playlists with the pieces from this book.

Comprehensive biography of Brahms.

Free eBook: *Romantic Composers*.

Resource links to books and internet sites.

Recommended recordings.